Wonders

Mc
Graw
Hill

mheducation.com/prek-12

Send all inquiries to:
McGraw Hill
1325 Avenue of the Americas
New York, NY 10019

ISBN: 978-1-26-581623-0
MHID: 1-26-581623-9

Printed in the United States of America.

4 5 6 7 8 9 LWI 26 25 24 23 22

A

Welcome to an Amazing Year of Reading!

This book is like a library in your hand. It is filled with different texts and stories by award-winning authors and illustrators. Let's read on to find out more.

Reading and Writing Through
Wonders

The more you read, the more you'll learn! You will spend time talking and writing about texts. You will explore how the books connect to you and your world.

Building Knowledge

Reading these texts will help you build knowledge about different topics. Each weekly text starts off with an **Essential Question**. This question helps you set a purpose for what you will learn from the text.

Genre Fantasy

Essential Question
How can we work together to make our lives better?

Read about how some smart cows and hens get what they want.

Click, Clack, Moo Cows That Type

by Doreen Cronin
illustrated by Betsy Lewin

270

271

Essential Question

Your New Learning Partners

This book and your **Reading/Writing Companion** are connected. They work together as your partners in reading, writing, and thinking.

Reading/Writing Companion

Literature Anthology

Once you learn new ideas, you will take that knowledge with you everywhere you go!

What You'll Read

You will find different types of texts, or genres, in this book. You will use what you learn about each genre in the Reading/Writing Companion to read these texts.

Realistic Fiction

FOLKTALE

Fantasy

Opinion Text

Nonfiction

PLAY

Poetry

Personal Narrative

Biography

Wonders

Amazing Stories

You will read wonderful fiction stories. The stories include realistic fiction, fantasies, and folktales. Follow the characters through these exciting stories.

Powerful Poetry

You will read different poems. As you read poetry, listen to the rhyme and rhythm that help you understand the meaning of each poem.

Interesting Nonfiction

There are different kinds of nonfiction texts. They all teach us facts about a topic. You will see special features in texts, such as maps and photographs. These help you build more knowledge.

Gallo Images-Daryl Balfour/Photodisc/Getty Images

Sneak Peek at the Stories and Poems

This year, you will read great stories and poems. They will help you see your world in new ways.

This year, you will read stories about friendship. In *Hi! Fly Guy* by **Tedd Arnold,** you'll read about how a pet can be a best friend. In *Lissy's Friends* by **Grace Lin,** you will read about a girl who makes new friends by sharing origami.

You will read stories about taking action. In *Rain School* by **James Rumford,** you'll read about children who build their own schoolhouse. In *Click, Clack, Moo: Cows That Type* by **Doreen Cronin**, you'll read about cows who want a better life on their farm.

You will read poems about family and friends. In *Abuelita's Lap* by **Pat Mora,** you'll read about a boy who spends time with his grandmother. In *There Are Days and There Are Days* by **Beatrice Schenk de Regniers,** you'll read about the fun you can have being with friends and by yourself, too.

You will read stories about exploring the world around you. In *Kitten's First Full Moon* by **Kevin Henkes,** you'll read about a curious kitten who wants to get to the Moon.

Sneak Peek at the Nonfiction Texts

Wonders is filled with texts that will help you build knowledge about science and social studies.

You will read texts about animals and how they survive in nature. In *Vulture View,* **April Pulley Sayre** tells how vultures use their bodies to find food.

You will read texts about history. In *Long Ago and Now* by **Minda Novek,** you'll learn about how things in the past were similar to or different from our lives today.

You will read about exploring the world. In *The Moon,* you'll read about how a telescope helps us see the Moon up close. In *Building Bridges,* you'll learn how engineers build different kinds of bridges.

You will learn about important issues. You will read about taking care of bees in **"Save Our Bees!"** and volunteering in **"Be a Volunteer!"** You will read the authors' opinions about the topics. This will help you form your own opinions.

The best way to learn about things that interest you is to do a lot of reading.

"Let's get reading!"

UNIT 2

Our Community

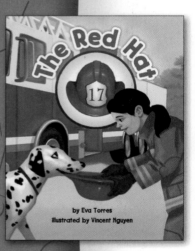

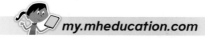

my.mheducation.com

4

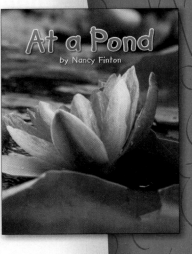
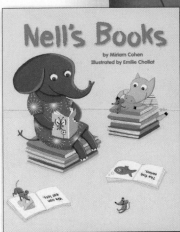

(t) Frans Lemmens/The Image Bank/Getty Images; (b) Ken Karp/McGraw Hill

Essential Question

What jobs need to be done in a community?

Read about a firefighter's exciting job.

Go Digital!

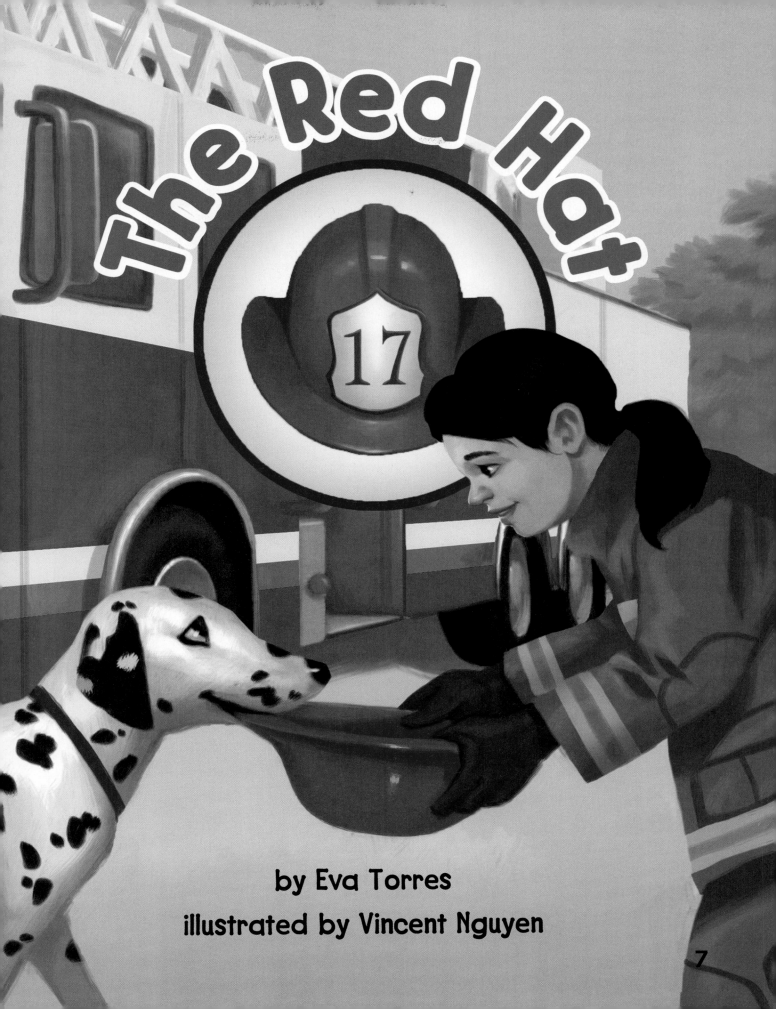

The Red Hat

by Eva Torres

illustrated by Vincent Nguyen

Jen has a **new** job.
She gets a red hat.

She will **use** this hat a lot.

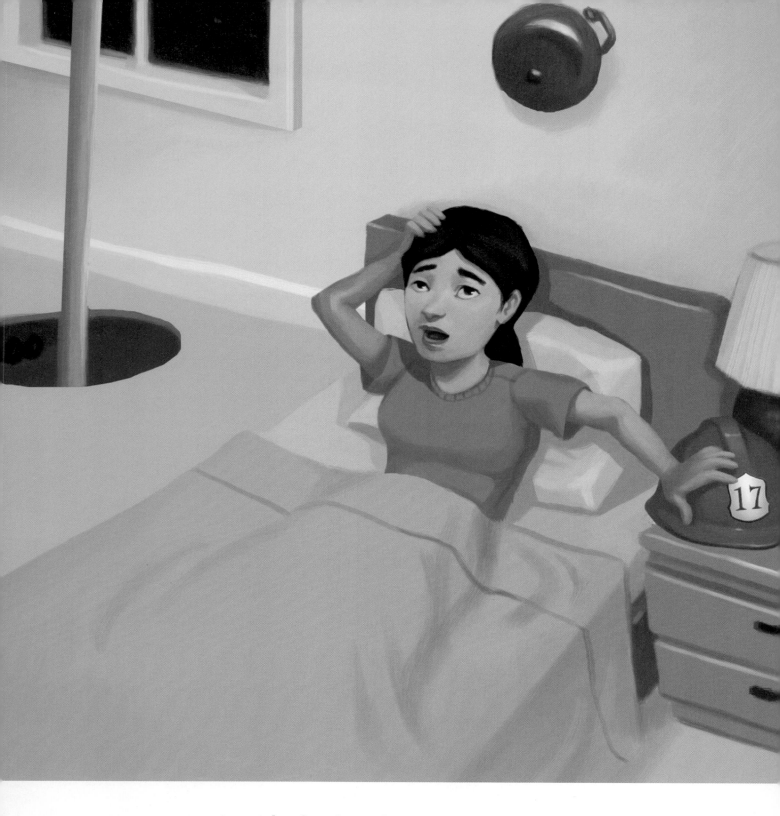

Jen is in bed.
There is a bell!
She grabs the red hat.

Jen can get down like this.
Go, Jen, go!

Jen hops on.
Go, Jen, go!

It is a big fire!
Jen can **help**.

The fire is out.
Jen is wet.
Thank you, Jen!

Jen plays with Matt and Jill.
There is a bell **again**.

Jen gets the red hat.
She gets in the truck.
Go, Jen, go!

Rex is up there.

He will not come to Jim.

Jen will help!

Jen gets Rex.

Jim is glad.

Rex is glad, too.

He has a new red bed.

Thank you, Jen!

Meet the Illustrator

Vincent Nguyen says, "I live near a firehouse in New York City, so I'm familiar with its sights and sounds. To illustrate *The Red Hat,* I just walked around the block and took photos that helped me draw the pictures."

Illustrator's Purpose

Vincent Nguyen wanted to show what the inside of a firehouse looks like. Draw something that is inside a firehouse. Label your picture.

Respond to the Text

Retell

Use your own words to retell *The Red Hat*. Tell who the characters are, where they are, and what happens to them.

Character	Setting	Events

Write

Would you like to have Jen's job? Tell why or why not. Include reasons for your opinion. Use these sentence starters:

I think Jen's job is...
I would like...

Make Connections

COLLABORATE

 How does Jen help her community?
ESSENTIAL QUESTION

Compare Texts

Read about what real firefighters do.

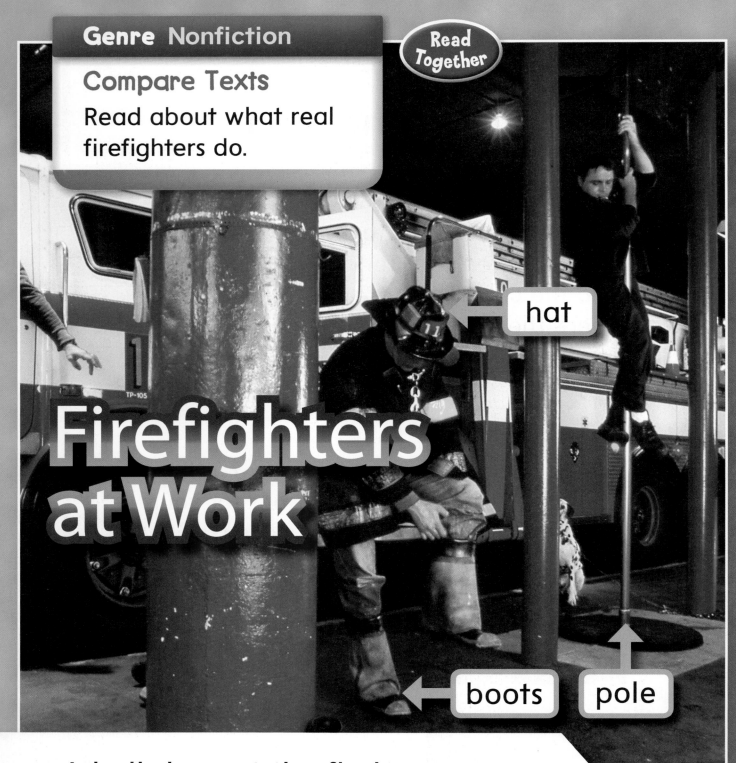

hat

boots

pole

Firefighters at Work

A bell rings at the firehouse.

Firefighters slide down a pole.

They put on special clothes fast!

Richard Hutchings/PhotoEdit

The firefighters jump in a fire truck.
The red truck speeds to the fire.
It has a loud **siren** and a flashing red
light. That tells cars to move away!

lights

ladder

hose

The brave firefighters get to work.
They use hoses to spray water.
Their special clothes **protect** them.
They put out the fire!

Now it is time for lunch.
They have lunch together.
Then they wait for the next bell.

Make Connections
How do firefighters help the community?
Essential Question

Richard Hutchings/PhotoEdit

25

26

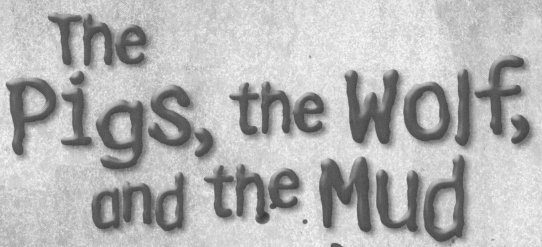

The Pigs, the Wolf, and the Mud

by Ellen Tarlow

illustrated by
Pablo Bernasconi

Three pigs **lived** in a mud hut.

"It is a mess," said Pig **One**.

"But pigs like a mess," said Pig Two.

"Mud is fun!" yelled Pig Three.

"Get this!" yelled Pig One.
She tossed mud to Pig Two.
"Mud is fun!" yelled Pig Three.

The bell rang.

"Little pigs, pigs, pigs, let me in."

"It is a big, bad wolf!" said Pig One.
"We can not let you in," yelled the
pigs. "You will eat us up."

"**Then** I will huff and puff,"
the wolf yelled back.
He huffed, huffed, huffed.
He puffed, puffed, puffed.

"Yuck!" said the wolf.
"I can not huff in mud.
I can not puff in mud."

He rang the bell again.
"Pigs, pigs, pigs, let me in!"
he yelled.
"We will not let you in!"
the pigs yelled back.

"Then I will kick, kick, kick,"
said the wolf.
He kicked, kicked, kicked.

The hut fell in!

"Yuck!" said the wolf.

"I can not look at this mud."

"You pigs are a big mess!"
"Yes!" yelled the pigs.
"Pigs like a big mess!"

"But I do not!" yelled the
wolf. "I must get this mud
off. Good-bye, pigs."

"Let's make a hut," said Pig One.
"We **could** use bricks," said Pig Two.
"We could use sticks," said Pig Three.

"We will use mud," said Pig One.
"Mud is good!" said Pig Two.
"Mud is fun!" yelled Pig Three.
"Yuck!" said the wolf.

Meet the Illustrator

Pablo Bernasconi loves illustrating animals doing funny things. Pablo's studio is a mess, full of junk and papers. But Pablo loves being surrounded by his things, just as the pigs in the story love being surrounded by mud.

Illustrator's Purpose

Pablo Bernasconi likes to draw funny animals. Draw and write about an animal doing something you think is funny.

Pablo Bernasconi

Respond to the Text

Retell

Use your own words to retell *The Pigs, the Wolf, and the Mud.* Tell who the characters are, where they are, and what happens to them.

Character	Setting	Events

Write

Should the pigs be worried that the wolf will come back to bother them? Why or why not? Use text evidence. Use these sentence starters:

The pigs should...
The wolf...

Make Connections

COLLABORATE

How is the pigs' hut like a building you know? How is it different?

ESSENTIAL QUESTION

Genre Nonfiction

Compare Texts
Read about the different
homes people make.

Read
Together

Homes Around the World

There are many kinds of **homes**.
People **build** their homes to fit
the place they live!

This home is built
into a rock.

44

This home is
made of wood.

This is a good home for a wet
place. There is a lot of water
here. The stilts help keep this
home dry.

This is a good home for a hot place.
There is a lot of clay in this place.
People use it to build homes. Clay
keeps the home cool inside.

©Sylvain Grandadam/Stone/Getty Images

This home is made of clay.

An igloo is made of ice.

There is a lot of ice in this place. People can use it to build. This is an igloo. People don't live in igloos. But they are good **shelter** from the cold.

What is your home like?

Make Connections
Which home do you think the pigs in *The Pigs, the Wolf, and the Mud* would like? Why? **Essential Question**

Essential Question

Where do animals live together?

Read about animals that live at a pond.

Go Digital!

Frans Lemmens/The Image Bank/Getty Images

48

At a Pond

by Nancy Finton

Who lives at a pond?

Who is **under** the water?
Who is on the land?
Who can fly to the pond?
Let's see!

Frogs live at a pond.

They swim and hop and jump.

Frogs rest on plants on the pond.

This frog is hunting for bugs.
It sees a bug.
Will it get a snack?
It has to be quick! Yum, yum!

(inset) David & Micha Sheldon/Fl Online/Getty Images; Nigel Dennis/Gallo Images/SuperStock

Ducks come to the pond.

They **eat** lots **of** bugs and plants.

This duck dips its bill to get bugs.

Dip, dip, dip!

Ducks make nests on land.

They use twigs and grass.

Who is in the eggs?

Quack, quack, quack!

Turtles can be on land and in water.

They swim and swim.

Then they stop and rest in the sun.

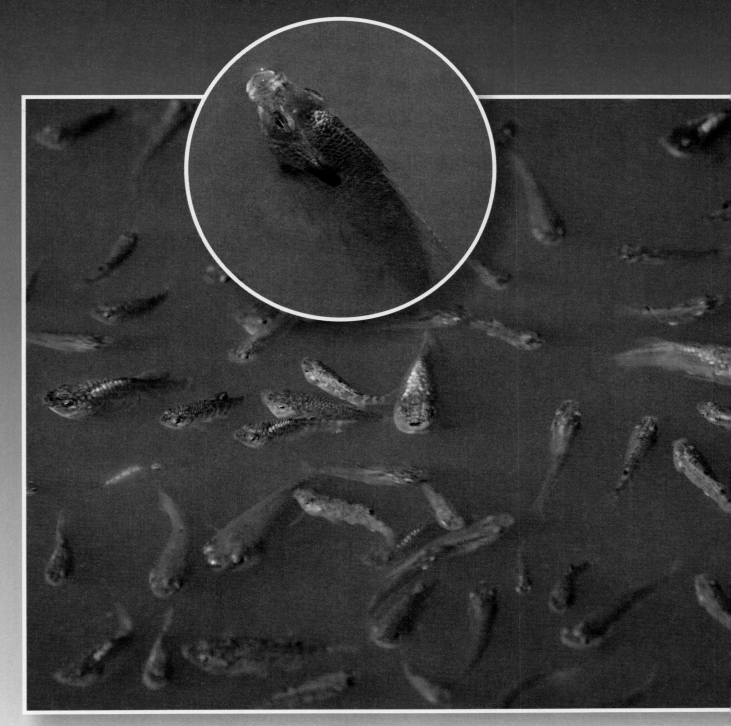

Can fish be on land? **No!**
Fish live in water.
They swim, swim, swim.
A big fish comes up to eat. Gulp!

(inset) ARCO/J. Meul/age fotostock; Jason Stemple. Reproduced with permission of Curtis Brown, Ltd.

Bugs like water.

Lots of bugs live at a pond.

A dragonfly is a big bug.

You can see it at a pond.

egret

raccoon

newt

goldfish

toad

beaver

Look at the animals at a pond.
Who are they?

Meet the Author

(tl) Nancy Finton; (bkgd) Reiner Goertner/Pixtal/Age fotostock

Nancy Finton says, "I love living and working in a big, busy city. But sometimes it feels too big and busy! Then I wish I were sitting by a quiet pond with the frogs and turtles."

Author's Purpose

Nancy Finton wanted to write about animals that live at a pond. She wanted readers to see the animals close up. Draw a place where animals live together. Write about your picture.

Respond to the Text

Retell

Use your own words to retell *At a Pond*. Information from your Author's Purpose chart may help you.

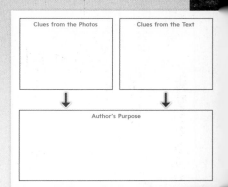

Clues from the Photos	Clues from the Text

Author's Purpose

Write

Write two more pages about one of the animals in *At a Pond*. Use the photos to help you. Use these sentence starters:

> This animal lives. . .
> This animal can. . .

Make Connections

COLLABORATE

How is the pond like the bayou in *Babies in the Bayou?*

ESSENTIAL QUESTION

Compare Texts

Read about animals that live in the water.

Read Together

Way Down Deep

by Mary Ann Hoberman

Underneath the water
Way down deep
In sand and stones and seaweed
Starfish creep
Snails inch slowly
Oysters sleep
Underneath the water
Way down deep.

Make Connections

How is under the sea like the pond? How is it different? **Essential Question**

Essential Question

How do people help out in the community?

Read about an elephant who loves books.

Go Digital!

The sun is hot.

Pig is big.

Nell's Books

by Miriam Cohen

Illustrated by Emilie Chollat

Nell liked to read.

She liked it a lot.

Nell could sit and read **all day** long.

"Will you play with us, Nell?"
called Cat and Dog.
"Shh!" said Nell. "I am reading."

67

"Will you shop with me, Nell?"
asked Pig.
"Shh!" said Nell. "This is good!"

"That Nell is not fun at all,"
said Dog.
"She just reads," said Cat.
"She will not do a thing!"

Then one day it rained.
Dog and Cat set up a tent.
Pig got dressed up for fun.
"This is good," said Dog.
"Yes!" said Pig and Cat.

It rained the next day, too.
"We **want** to go out," said Dog.
"We are sick of tents and dressing up,"
said Pig and Cat.

Nell went to **her** shelf.

"Here, Dog," she said.

"I think you will like this."

"Yuck!" said Dog.

72

"This will be fun for Pig," said Nell.
"Cat, you will like this a lot."
"Ick!" said Cat and Pig.
"Shh!" said Nell. "Let's read."

73

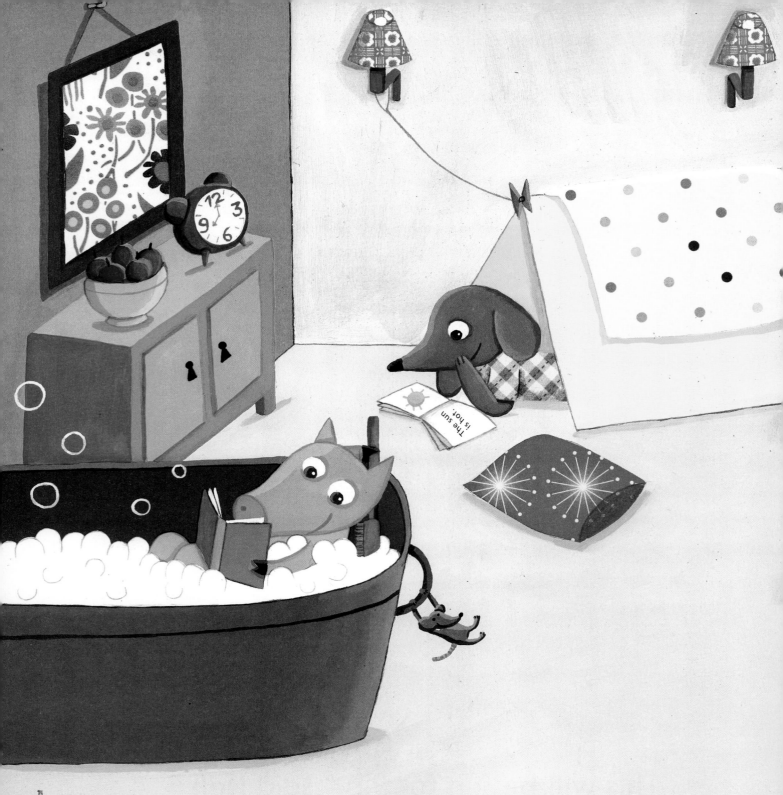

Dog read in his tent.
Pig read in a tub.
Cat read in a pot.

They read all day long.
"This is fun!" said Cat
and Dog and Pig.

The next day, Nell heard clanging.
She heard banging.
"Nell, come quick!" called Dog.

"We did this for you," said Dog.
"You can hand out books to all,"
said Cat.
"Nell is good at that," said Pig.
"That is just my wish!" said Nell.

Nell got in.
"Let's hand out books," she said.

"Shh!" said Dog and Cat and Pig.
"Let us read!"

Meet the Author

Miriam Cohen says, "I have always loved elephants because they are smart animals that do nice things for other elephants. I imagined an elephant that was so smart she could read. I had fun writing about how she shared her love of books with her friends."

Author's Purpose

Miriam Cohen wanted to tell about an animal that helps its community. Draw an animal helping its community. Write about it.

Miriam Cohen

Respond to the Text

Retell

Use your own words to retell *Nell's Books*. Tell who the characters are, where they are, and what happens to them.

Character	Setting	Events

Write

Extend the story to tell what Nell might do next. Use these sentence starters:

Nell wants to...
Her friends help by...

Make Connections

COLLABORATE

How does giving books out help a community?

ESSENTIAL QUESTION

Compare Texts

Read about how kids can help out.

Kids Can Help!

How can kids help the **neighborhood**?

Kids can help grow a **garden**! It is fun to plant seeds and help them grow.

A community garden is a great
place to help. The plants are pretty
to look at. And everyone can enjoy
fresh fruits and vegetables.

Kids can help clean the playground. They can pick up trash. They can **recycle** cans and bottles.

Recycling makes the neighborhood clean. Recycling helps our Earth, too.

Do you want to help your neighborhood? Think about what you can do.

How We Can Help

1. Plant a garden.

2. Clean the playground.

3. Recycle cans and bottles.

Make Connections

How does a garden help a community? **Essential Question**

Essential Question

How can you find your way around?

Learn how to use a map.

Go Digital!

A map is a drawing of a **place**.
A map shows us where we are.
It shows us how to get **around**, too.

Phil's Room

A map can be of a small place.

This is a map of Phil's room.

How **many** windows do you see?

What is next to Phil's bed?

What is **by** the door?

A map can be of a big place.
This is a map of a town.
What places do you see on
the map?

Which street is the market on?

What is by the firehouse?

How would you **walk** from the
school to the library?

A map can be of a fun place.
This is a map of a park.
The symbols on maps stand for real
things. On this map,  stands for
a place to eat lunch.

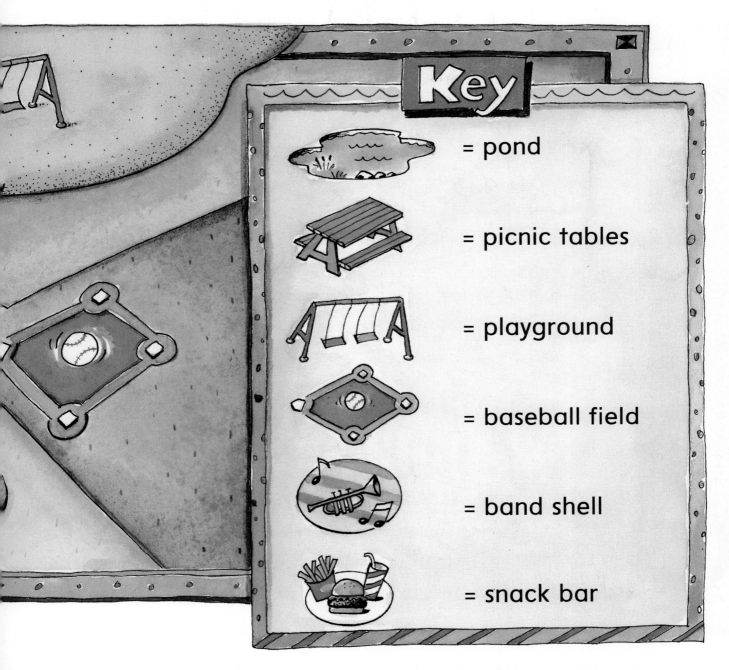

A key tells what the symbols mean.
Match the symbol in the key with
the one on the map.
What symbol stands for the pond?
What does stand for?

A map can be of an imaginary place.
This is a treasure map.
What routes could you take to get
to the chest of gold? This map could
help you a lot!

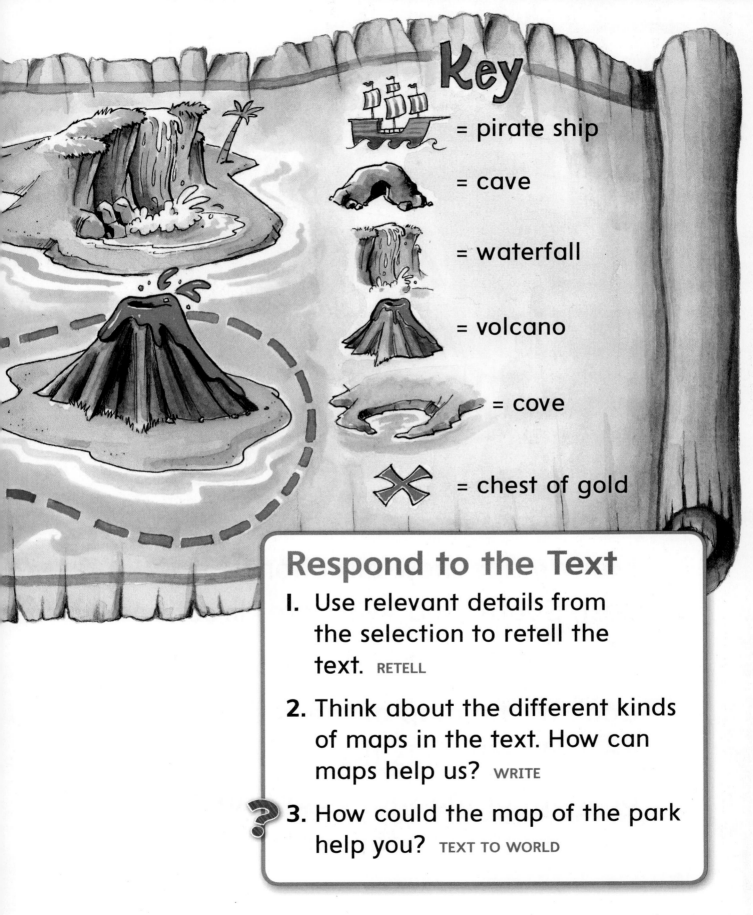

Key

= pirate ship

= cave

= waterfall

= volcano

= cove

= chest of gold

Respond to the Text

1. Use relevant details from the selection to retell the text. RETELL

2. Think about the different kinds of maps in the text. How can maps help us? WRITE

3. How could the map of the park help you? TEXT TO WORLD

North, East, South, or West?

Many maps show directions. North,
East, South, and West are directions.
Directions tell us which way to go.

Look at the map of the zoo. Find
each direction. Is the lion north
or south of the snack bar? Are the
chimps closer to the east or west?

Illustration: Steven Mach

94

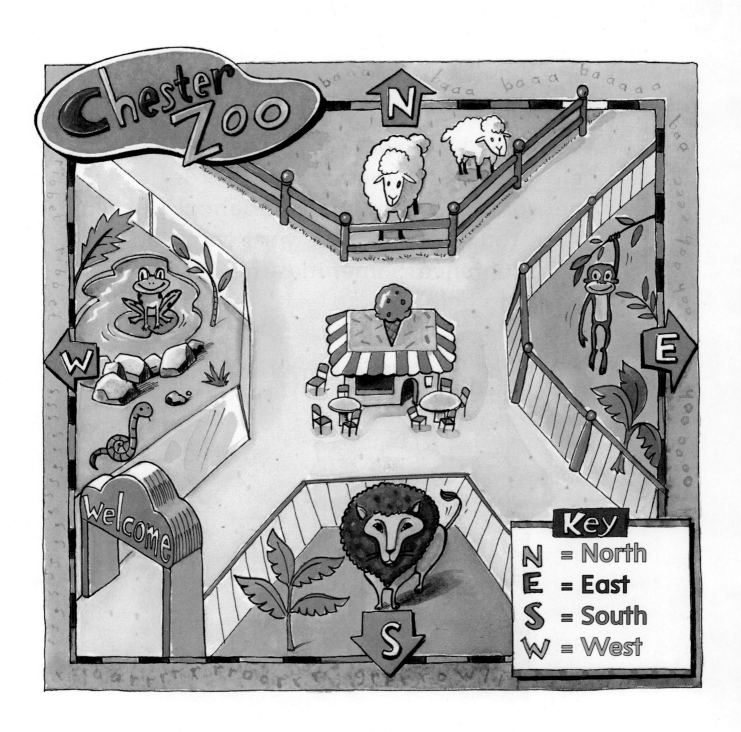

Make Connections

 What is north of the baseball field on the map of Bell Park?

Essential Question

Glossary

What is a Glossary? A glossary can help you find the meanings of words. The words are listed in alphabetical order. You can look up a word and read it in a sentence. Sometimes there is a picture to help you.

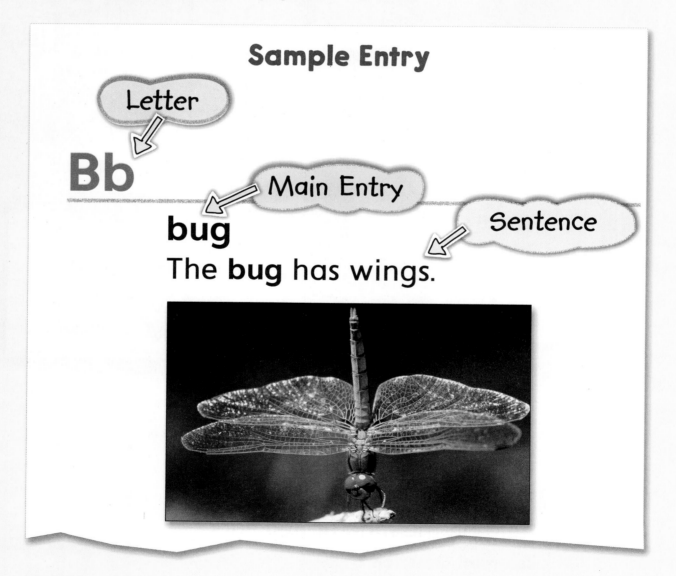

Sample Entry

Letter

Bb

Main Entry

bug

Sentence

The **bug** has wings.

Bb

book

It is good to read a **book**.

bug

The **bug** has wings.

Ee

eat

Jess can **eat** an apple.

Jj

job

A vet has a fun **job**.

Ll

lunch

This is a good **lunch**.

Mm

mess

This room is a **mess**.

(t) Jupiterimages/Comstock Images/Getty Images; (b) Ash Lindsey Photography/Flickr/Getty Images

mud

The pigs are in the **mud**.

Nn

new

Jim is getting **new** shoes.

Pp

pond

Ducks swim in the **pond**.

Rr

red

The truck is **red**.

Ss

shelf

The books are on the **shelf**.

Tt

tent

We can sleep in a **tent**.

three

Three frogs sit.

Ww

walk

The friends **walk** together.